ARE YOU F.A.T ?

FAITHFUL - AVAILABLE – TEACHABLE

R. DAVE JONES

ISBN: 9798339590842

Cover design and formatting by Karl V. Perry, KPGraphics

Published by R. Dave Jones Ministries

Printed in the United States

DEDICATION

This book is dedicated to the memory of those who have profoundly helped shape my life and contributed to the realization of this project. Some of whom are no longer with us, their influence, love, and guidance continue to inspire me.

Robyn Gool – The late *Pastor, Victory Christian Center, Charlotte, N.C.*

A Pastor's Pastor! For his unwavering walk of faith before all who had the pleasure of being a part of what God was doing with his life. Unselfish service and sharing of everything God had set to his charge. The Body of Christ needs more leaders of this caliper. Pastor Gool was F.A.T. to me.

Jimmie Lee Smith – The late Archbishop, *Light of the World International and Light of the World Christian Tabernacle, Stockbridge, GA.*

Bishop Smith extended opportunity after opportunity to me to exercise the ministry God had placed within me. Not only around singing and preaching, but also allowed me to develop evangelistic outreach and senior members ministries. He placed trust in me during my season of uncertainty. I shall forever be thankful.

Clint Jones – The late *Pastor, Greater Salvation B.C., New Orleans, La.*

I will always remember the long nights around his kitchen table talking about the things of God and the Word of God. It was Pastor Jones who first noticed the hand of God upon my life when I was too immature to see for myself. It was under his ministry that I was given the responsibility of Sunday School Superintendent. Thanks for seeding my Love for the Word of God.

Edward and Lucendia Jones – *My parents*

They were the nurturers of my "steadfastness" within the Body of Christ. I watched them serve the people of God without "murmuring and complaining." I believe they nurtured that in their children. Consistently, no matter what was happening in their personal lives, their service to God through the people of God was paramount. I gratefully Love you guys for your example.

Jones Family – *At Large*

I am constantly reminded of the tremendous giftings, callings, and trust God has seemingly always placed within this Family. If we are not known by others for anything else, we are known for our relationship(s) with God. To that I say, #JONESSTRONG #Glory to God!

ACKNOWLEDGMENTS

I am deeply grateful to everyone who contributed to this project. This project would not have been possible without the support, dedication, and hard work of my incredible team members.

Beatrice F. Jones
Serena J. Dorsey
Sonya S. Jones
Nia S. Thompson
Danielle N. Palmer
Dorian D. Starks
Loretta A. Richardson
Lisa S. Webb
Sirai Thomas
Reese Wright
Dr. Sam Chand
Dr. Josie Carr
Bishop Karl V. Perry, Sr.
Dr. D'Ann V. Johnson
Archbishop Ruth W. Smith
Pastor Dexter Kilgore
Dr. Terry & Elder Anita Richardson
Dr. Vanessa Anderson

To all of you I owe a debt of gratitude for your selfless dedication to this project. Each one of you are F.A.T., and it would have been incomplete without you.

I Love my Team!

With deepest appreciation,
R. Dave Jones

FOREWORD

Have you noticed, that on almost every book best-seller list there always are books about cooking, diet, weight loss. They focus on diets, health and wellness, quick hacks to weight loss, longer life, recipes and the latest fads on nutrition.

My friend Dave Jones wants you to be FAT!

FAT is good.

Faithful. **A**vailable. **T**eachable.

Church leaders bemoan the fact that it is harder today than ever to have people who are faithful, available and teachable. This deficiency is creating an anemic and hollow church.

From the outside looking in it seems that people are there, worship and music is strong, preaching is anointed and other indicators are good. But, when it comes to Christian maturity leading to serving others selflessly without expectations of positions, power and prestige the church is hollow.

Lots of church members and attendees. Even a good number of Christians. But, disciples? That number dwindles dramatically. Being FAT differentiates Christians from Disciples.

Allow me to break it down with a brutal question for all Pastors: "What percentage of the people who come to your church would you consider FAT disciples?"

Christians grow into disciples by being *faithful*.

Faithful to the Word. Faithful in worship. Faithful in generous stewardship. Faithful in witnessing. Faithful in living a holy life of integrity. Faithful in honoring those who serve you spiritually. *Faithful*.

Christians grow into disciples by being *available*.

Available when it is inconvenient. Available when you don't get the credit. Available even when it's not your responsibility. Available to people and areas of service you don't like. *Available*.

Christians grow into disciples by being *teachable*.

Teachable when you know it all already. Teachable when it is a different thought than you're accustomed to. Teachable when the Spirit wants to do "a new thing". *Teachable*.

The question still persists: "Are you FAT?"

Sam Chand
Leadership Consultant and author of Leadership Pain

FOREWORD

Most people want their lives to count for something significant in the Kingdom of God as well as in their personal lives. In this riveting masterpiece, "Are You F.A.T.", Pastor R. Dave Jones lays out a viable blueprint that will move you from status quo mediocrity to living the more abundant life authentically in God as a **F**aithful, **A**vailable and **T**eachable person.

The irony of the question "Are you FAT?" adds humor to the text initially but as Pastor Jones clearly delineates its meaning, it becomes thought-provoking and leads the reader on a path of soul searching and self-discovery. As a Believer, are **you** Faithful? Are **you** Available? And...are **you** Teachable?

I have known Pastor Jones for most of his life and have witnessed his development and strong resolve in the things of God. This book is a heart-warming expression of his love for God's people and his desire to see you reach your highest potential.

Being F.A.T. is a prerequisite to experiencing the manifested blessings of God in your life and will deliver the results you expect time after time again. If you want to be the best you can be, get FAT! If you want to be a positive example to others, get FAT! If you want your light to shine brighter, get FAT! If you want to be used in a greater capacity in ministry, get FAT!

I highly recommend this book to you and others like you. Allow it to serve as a resource that will support and aid your journey in becoming a more valuable asset in ministry, your personal life and career.

To God be the glory and much success to you!

Josie Carr, Ed. D.
DESTINY Educational Consulting
CEO/Senior Consultant
Author: The Power of Confidence, A Framework to Your Success

Pastor's Blurbs

Are You F.A.T.?

Packed into a slim physique is a man who has always been F.A.T. In his practical and no-nonsense style, Dave Jones helps us recognize and develop the qualities of faithfulness, availability, and being teachable, and gives us an action plan for how to use these traits to add value as we serve in our various contexts.

Dr. D'Ann V. Johnson
Executive Pastor, New Covenant Christian Ministries
Founder, Overflow Ministries International

This approach is extremely practical and powerful. Anyone interested in being healthy in your professional personal life using these three tools are a must. For anyone looking to grow F.A.T is the model to follow. Pastor Dave Jones has provided for us the ingredients to grow and develop.

Pastor Dexter Kilgore
Senior Pastor
World Restoration Church

In a culture where many of us are weight conscious, it is a little different to consider one's self FAT. Pastor R. Dave Jones gives FAT an entirely different meaning.

He poses the question, "are you FAT?" When one looks closer at his meaning, perhaps we all want to be FAT: FAITHFUL, AVAILABLE AND TEACHABLE.

This is a must read for all leaders who are ready to go to the NEXT!

Dr. Ruth W. Smith
Archbishop
Light of the World Covenant Fellowship

Pastor Dave Jones has written a work addressing a prevalent but rarely discussed topic in society as a whole and specifically in the faith community. Pastor Jones' insight and attention to the topic of F.A.T. (Faithful, Available, and Teachable) is very profound and so appropriate in light of a society that is becoming more and more self-centered. This book reveals the obvious principles while unveiling some hidden truths that all who read them will appreciate and value. Pastor Jones' commitment to this project will prove to be a blessing to the reader.

Bishop Dr. Terry and Elder Anita Richardson
Christian Growth Ministries, Inc.

I endorse the author... R. Dave Jones is a dynamic teacher of the word who uses life examples to illustrate spiritual truths.

Dr. Vanessa Anderson

Minister of Education
Covenant Christian Ministries

CONTENTS

INTRODUCTION

What if the key to unlocking a life of purpose, fulfilment, and divine destiny lies hidden within three simple letters? What if these letters held the secret to experiencing the abundant life promised in the Bible?

In a world fraught with uncertainty, where chaos seems to reign supreme and the clamor of distractions grows ever louder, a clarion call echoes through the ages, beckoning us to pause, to listen, to ponder: Are You F.A.T.?

This isn't a question of physical stature or dietary habits. No, it delves far deeper, probing the recesses of the soul, and challenging the very core of our being. It asks us to confront our faithfulness, our availability, and our capacity to be teachable – three pillars upon which the edifice of our existence stands and upon which our success in life can be guaranteed.

God desires that we be blessed in all areas of our lives, however, we see many Christians, lovers of God, and those whom God love, struggling in life. It is normal to ask WHY?

In the pages of this book, you will embark on a transformative journey, guided by timeless wisdom and ancient truths, as you explore the principles of faithfulness, availability, and teachableness. You will know the Why. Prepare to be challenged, to be stretched, to be stirred from complacency as you traverse the sacred landscapes of scripture and the depths of your own heart.

If you follow the teachings of Jesus in the Bible, you will understand how God blesses men, you will understand how God's kingdom functions, and you will understand that being F.A.T. is the foundation for receiving the ever-increasing blessings of God.

As we journey, it becomes evident that the vitality of organizations, groups, businesses, churches, and families hinges on the contributions of individuals embodying the core principles of FAT.

Through the stories of biblical heroes and heroines, you will witness the power of faithfulness to overcome adversity, the courage of availability to seize divine opportunities, and the humility of being teachable to unlock the treasures of wisdom hidden in the depths of eternity.

But beware, this journey is not for the faint of heart or those consumed by selfish ambitions. It demands courage, conviction, and a willingness to confront the shadows lurking within. Yet, in the crucible of trial and tribulation, you will discover the radiant truth that has illuminated the path of seekers for thousands of years.

True fulfilment, true success, true abundance – they await those who dare to ask themselves the question: Am I F.A.T.? So, I implore you to turn the pages and to embark on this odyssey of self-discovery and divine encounter. For within these words lies the promise of a life transformed, a destiny fulfilled, and a legacy etched in the annals of eternity.

CHAPTER 1

UNMASKING FAITHFULNESS

James 2:14, 26 (NIV)
14 What good is it, my brothers and sisters, if someone claims to have faith but has no deeds? Can such faith save them?
26 As the body without the spirit is dead, so faith without deeds is dead.

Faithfulness is continuous, unrelenting loyalty and commitment.

If you follow closely the teachings of Jesus in the Bible, you will learn how the kingdom of God functions. The blessings of God come upon the life of a man in levels (stage by stage). The criterion for each next level is **faithfulness** at the present level.

Jesus in *Matthew 25:14-30 (NIV)* was teaching on the parable of the talents. In this parable, the master gave three of his servants' talents according to their abilities. Let's read the parable. Pay attention to the texts with bold fonts.

*14 "Again, it will be like a man going on a journey, who called his servants and entrusted his wealth to them. 15 To one he gave five bags of gold, to another two bags, and to another one bag, **each according to his ability.** Then he went on his journey. 16 The man who had received five bags of gold went at once and put his money to work and gained five bags more. 17 So also, the one with two bags of gold gained two more. 18 But the man who had received one bag went off, dug a hole in the ground and hid his master's money.*

*19 "**After a long time** the master of those servants returned and settled accounts with them. 20 The man who had received five bags of gold brought the other five. 'Master,' he said, 'you entrusted me with five bags of gold. See, I have gained five more.'*

*21 "His master replied, '**Well done**, good and **faithful** servant! You have been **faithful** with a few things; **I will put you in charge of many things.** Come and share your master's happiness!'*

22 "The man with two bags of gold also came. 'Master,' he said, 'you entrusted me with two bags of gold; see, I have gained two more.'

23 "His master replied, 'Well done, good and faithful servant! You have been faithful with a few things; I will put you in charge of many things. Come and share your master's happiness!'

24 "Then the man who had received one bag of gold came. 'Master,' he said, 'I knew that you are a hard man, harvesting where you have not sown and gathering where you have not scattered seed. 25 So I was afraid and went out and hid your gold in the ground. See, here is what belongs to you.'

26 "His master replied, 'You wicked, lazy servant! So you knew that I harvest where I have not sown and gather where I have not scattered seed? 27 Well then, you should have put my money on deposit with the bankers, so that when I returned I would have received it back with interest.

28 "So take the bag of gold from him and give it to the one who has ten bags. 29 For whoever has will be given more, and they will have an abundance. Whoever does not have, even what they have will be taken from them. 30 And throw that worthless servant outside, into the darkness, where there will be weeping and gnashing of teeth.'

From the scripture above, there is a lot to learn. The master in the parable is God, you and I represent the servants, and the talents mentioned is anything God entrusted into our hands (money, influence, spiritual gifts, wisdom, skills and talents, relationships, our marriage, our children, your subordinates, if you are in leadership, etc.).

One important thing we should note is that the master gave them talents according to their abilities. It was not based on their prayer points or hard work. So, the extent to which God will bless us is dependent on our ability, and our capacity during the season in which we find ourselves. The servants were not given equal talents. At the end of the story, you would realize that it was a wise decision by the master – each of them functioned according to their ability. Howbeit if the 5 talents were given to the guy who received 1 talent – the master would have wasted his resources.

We need to understand that for everything God gives us, he expects us to make a profit out of it, increase it and use it judiciously.

In verse 19, the Bible says, *"After a long time…"* God gives us time to use all that he has given us, and he will always return to us periodically for us to give an account of what we have done with what he gave us. The question is "Will he count you faithful?"

When the master returned, to the faithful ones, he said to them *"Well done, good and faithful servant."* He did not stop there but he also gave them more. No matter what you do, no matter how much you pray, you are not qualified for more until you prove yourself faithful with what God has given you. This is not only applicable in our dealings with God, but it is also applicable in our dealings with men. No boss will promote a worker who has not done well and is faithful in his present position.

Wherever you find faithful people, they are considered assets.

Let us engage in a contemplative moment. Are you, in essence, an asset or a liability in the spheres of your home, workplace, or church community? Introspection into whether you contribute as an asset, facilitate progress, or stand as a liability hindering growth, is a crucial step. Shedding the superficial layers, let's start from within. Consider the fundamental question – how much do you genuinely like and love yourself? Are you faithful to the promises you make, or have you found yourself neglecting the commitments you've made to yourself?

In the retrospection of the past year, did you witness the manifestation of the plans you earnestly crafted? Were you, in essence, faithful to yourself? The evaluation of your habits, behaviors, and overall conduct becomes imperative. Do these elements contribute positively to your personal growth, or do they stagnate your progress?

Let us collectively embark on a profound exploration into the very definition of what it means to be an asset.

An **asset**, within the F.A.T paradigm, is not merely a valuable individual or resource. It transcends into an embodiment of Faithfulness, Availability, and Teachableness – a reservoir of **qualities that extend far beyond the present moment, with the anticipation of yielding future benefits**. Whether in the personal, spiritual, or business domain, assets are individuals who not only exhibit faithfulness but also exhibit the trait of availability and possess the capacity to impart wisdom.

Consider the analogy of a businessperson. A business asset, in the context of being F.A.T., is a beacon of value to the company. They contribute to the production of goods and services, drive growth, and epitomize the essence of being F.A.T. Conversely, individuals who fail to contribute positively might find themselves labeled as liabilities. This principle extends to the realms of churches and families.

Within the intricate dynamics of church and family life, assets can take on tangible or intangible forms. Tangible assets actively engage in daily responsibilities, playing a pivotal role in the holistic well-being of the group. On the other hand, intangible assets, exemplified by qualities like love, become the invisible threads binding individuals together.

Dennis Waitley's profound observation resonates deeply – *"Time and health are two precious assets that we don't recognize and appreciate until they have become depleted."* When these assets are managed with the characteristics of being F.A.T., their value magnifies.

However, on the flip side of this intricate dance between assets and liabilities, there emerges a stark reality. A **liability**, in its essence, **is someone or something likely to put one at a disadvantage.** It becomes a disruptive force, causing impediments to success. The imperative then is to surround oneself with individuals embodying the characteristics of being F.A.T. As you delve into your quiet moments, evaluate those around you – are they contributing as assets or hindering progress as liabilities?

As we venture deeper into the exploration of the essence of being F.A.T., let us again focus our attention on the first component: **faithfulness**. Faithfulness, within the F.A.T. context, extends beyond a mere suggestion; it is a fundamental requirement. It is a description of **actions** – remaining loyal and steadfast in the face of challenges and triumphs alike.

Drawing inspiration from the parable in Matthew 25, where servants are entrusted with talents according to their abilities, we witness the celebration of those who multiply their talents. They are hailed as not just being good, **but faithful.** The unfaithful one, however, faces consequences. It is not enough to only learn the benefits of being faithful, it is also important to know that unfaithfulness has its consequences. When the master returns and finds you unfaithful, you will not only remain at the same level, but you will possibly lose what you have right now (the experience of the consequence).

Faithfulness is not a mere suggestion; it is essential and demanded of stewards. As stewards of God's blessings, being faithful and trustworthy is not an option but a requirement. Charles Stanley astutely points out that many *"Christians commit convenience. They remain faithful as long as it is safe and doesn't involve risk, rejection, or criticism."* To gain experience and strength, we must be faithful in small things, as our strength and growth lie in them.

In life, the quest is not to find better values but to remain faithful to the ones that are dear to us. *1 Corinthians 4:2 (NIV) "Now it is required that those who have been given a trust must prove faithful."* Stewards must be found faithful and trustworthy, making it an essential requirement. Let us not be like the unfaithful servant who was given one talent. No matter how small or minute you think what you have now is, no matter how undersized your present level is, remember that it is someone's prayer point. So, be grateful to God, remain faithful, treasure what you have now, manage it well, and then you will be ready for more.

Let the journey into the essence of faithfulness be a beacon guiding us through the journey of life.

CHAPTER 2

FAITHFUL (LOYAL AND RELIABLE)

"Faithful servants never retire. You can retire from your career, but you will never retire from serving God."
(Rick Warren)

Our journey into understanding F.A.T. people, individuals embodying Faithfulness, Availability, and the ability to be Teachable, takes us deeper into the realms of faithfulness. In this chapter, we embark on a basic exploration of faithfulness, recognizing its nature and the profound impact it can have on various aspects of our lives.

Faithfulness is a cornerstone of the F.A.T. framework. It extends beyond the confines of religious commitments. It is a comprehensive virtue that permeates the fabric of our existence. Our commitment to faithfulness resonates not only in our spiritual pursuits but also in our interactions within the intricate tapestry of family, friendships, and professional commitments.

Loyalty: A Familiar Term

Let's investigate the meaning of faithfulness. The term 'loyalty' emerges as a familiar descriptor. Loyal individuals are *those who steadfastly provide firm and unwavering support*. While some may find solace in the term 'loyalty,' others might perceive 'faithfulness' as an overtly spiritual attribute. This linguistic distinction, does not diminish, but enhances, the essence of the underlying commitment.

Recognizing Loyalty

The ability to express and recognize loyalty often hinges on personal experiences. For those whose life's journey has been devoid of loyalty in different relationships, grasping its essence and articulating it becomes a formidable task. The absence of such experiences renders individuals unable to authentically express and embody loyalty.

Appreciating Predictability

One of the hallmarks of loyalty is predictability. Predictable individuals, like the unwavering hands of a clock, instill a sense of trust. In a world characterized by constant change, predictability becomes a rare and cherished virtue. Those who remain constant over time, un-swayed by external influences, become beacons of reliability and trustworthiness.

Turning to biblical narratives, the story of Ruth unfolds as a poignant testament to loyalty. Ruth's pledge to her mother-in-law transcends family ties, embodying a loyalty that defies conventional expectations. Her commitment to accompanying her mother-in-law, and adopt to her people and God, encapsulates a loyalty that surpasses the ordinary.

In the context of loyalty, predictability emerges as a virtue rather than a limitation. It is a quality that fosters trust and reliability. A predictable person becomes a dependable anchor in the tumultuous sea of life, offering reassurance and steadfastness.

Examining the biblical narrative of Peter, we encounter a momentary lapse in loyalty. Despite his initial assertion of unwavering loyalty, Peter denies Jesus three times!

Matthew 26:69-75 (NIV) 69 "Now Peter was sitting out in the courtyard, and a servant girl came to him. "You also were with Jesus of Galilee," she said. 70 But he denied it before them all. "I don't know what you're talking about," he said. 71 Then he went out to the gateway, where another servant girl saw him and said to the people there, "This fellow was with Jesus of Nazareth." 72 He denied it again, with an oath: "I don't know the man!" 73 After a little while, those standing there went up to Peter and said, "Surely you are one of them; your accent gives you away."

74 Then he began to call down curses, and he swore to them, "I don't know the man!" Immediately a rooster crowed. 75 Then Peter remembered the word Jesus had spoken: "Before the rooster crows, you will disown me three times." And he went outside and wept bitterly." This episode underscores the human struggle with faithfulness and the **potential for growth and redemption found in loyalty.**

Imperfect individuals, bound by loyalty, find perfection in the eyes of those they are loyal to. Loyalty transforms flaws into endearing qualities, fostering a sense of perfection within relationships. Imperfect people, when bound by the thread of loyalty, become perfect in each other's eyes if they are bound by that same level of loyalty.

Expanding our exploration, we can unravel additional terms closely related to faithfulness: being true, steadfast, and reliable. **"True"** signifies alignment with reality, emphasizing the need for actions to harmonize with expectations. **"Steadfastness"** involves resolute firmness and dutiful commitment, and **"Reliable"** refers to being consistently good in quality or performance, as illustrated through Daniel's unwavering decision not to defile himself.

Daniel 1:8 (NIV) *"But Daniel resolved not to defile himself with the royal food and wine, and he asked the chief official for permission not to defile himself this way."*

Renewing the Mind for Faithfulness

The concept of renewing the mind emerges as crucially important in maintaining faithfulness. Drawing inspiration from Paul's teachings in **Romans 12:2 (NIV) *"Do not conform to the pattern of this world, but be transformed by the renewing of your mind.*** Then you will be able to test and approve what God's will is—his good, pleasing and perfect will."

Spiritual maturity involves aligning one's mindset with godly values and ethical attitudes. The transformation of the mind becomes a prerequisite for ensuring that our actions authentically reflect the reality of faithfulness.

Reliability: The Measure of Trust

Reliability, often appreciated in others, is examined not merely as an external trait but as a personal commitment to keeping promises and consistently delivering high-quality performance. The Bible underscores the value of reliability in guiding and blessing the faithful *(Deut. 28);*

(Ps. 119:105). It is not merely a virtue appreciated by others but a characteristic that transforms one into a trustworthy and dependable individual.

Proverbs 28:20 (NIV) echoes the abundant blessings bestowed upon the faithful, it says, *"A faithful person will be richly blessed, but one eager to get rich will not go unpunished!"*

Being faithful over seemingly trivial commitments promises greater rewards. The journey of faithfulness is not a destination but a continuous process of personal growth and the potential to inspire and uplift others.

Are you faithful? Don't wait for someone else to evaluate you. Examine yourself. People will see your consistency, your loyalty and your reliability. Even when you are considered "predictable," take it as a compliment.

FAITHFULNESS IS GOOD!

Selah

1. In what areas of your life do you feel called to be more faithful?

2. How do your daily actions reflect your commitment to staying true to your values and beliefs?

3. When was the last time you were tempted to give up on something important? How did you handle it?

CHAPTER 3

AVAILABILITY

Philippians 2:3-4 (NIV)

3 Do nothing out of selfish ambition or vain conceit. Rather, in humility value others above yourselves, 4 not looking to your own interests but each of you to the interests of the others.

Being available is a fundamental principle that underpins our ability to benefit from the opportunities and blessings that life presents us. It's about more than just physical presence; it's a state of readiness, and a willingness to engage with the world around us and seize the possibilities that come our way. In essence, availability is the key that unlocks the door to progress and fulfillment in every aspect of our lives. Without it, we risk missing out on the countless blessings that await us, and opportunities that await us along our journey.

Consider, for a moment, the promises of God. They are abundant and overflowing, but they are of no use to us if we do not make ourselves available to receive them. It's not enough just for these promises to exist; we must position ourselves in such a way that we can access them and allow them to manifest in our lives. This requires a deliberate choice on our part—to open ourselves up to the possibilities that God has in store for us, and to align our actions with His will. When we do so, we pave the way for His blessings to flow freely into our lives.

Throughout history, God has consistently called people not based on their abilities, but on their availability. Consider figures like David, a humble shepherd boy who was anointed king, or Joseph, a slave who rose to become a ruler in Egypt. In both cases, their ascent to greatness was not due to their inherent skills or talents, but rather their willingness to make themselves available to God's plan. Similarly, in our own lives, we may feel inadequate or unqualified for the tasks set before us, but when we make ourselves available to God, He equips us with everything we need to succeed.

Being available means more than just being physically present; it's about being fully engaged and ready to contribute. Whether it's in our jobs, our communities, or our relationships, availability requires a willingness to step up and take responsibility. It means showing up not only with our bodies but also with our hearts and minds, ready to do whatever is needed to make a positive impact. This attitude of availability is what sets us apart and enables us to make a difference in the world around us.

In today's fast-paced world, it's easy to become overwhelmed and distracted by the demands of daily life. We may find ourselves constantly juggling commitments and struggling to find time for ourselves, let alone others. But amidst the chaos, it's essential to remember the importance of being available—to God, to our loved ones, and to ourselves. By making ourselves available, we open ourselves up to new opportunities and experiences, allowing us to grow and flourish in ways we never thought possible.

The COVID-19 pandemic has brought this principle of availability into sharp focus, forcing us to adapt to new ways of living and interacting with one another. In the face of uncertainty and adversity, we have been called upon to make ourselves available in ways we never imagined— whether it's by wearing masks, practicing social distancing, or supporting those in need. In doing so, we have demonstrated the resilience and strength that comes from being available to one another, even in the most challenging of times.

Ultimately, being available is not just about what we can receive, but also what we can give. It's about showing up for others, offering a listening ear, a helping hand, or a word of encouragement when they need it most. It's about being present and attentive, ready to offer our time, our resources, and ourselves for the greater good. In this way, availability becomes not only a pathway to personal fulfillment but also a catalyst for positive change in the world around us.

As we navigate the complexities of life, let us remember the power of availability—to open doors, to bridge divides, and to bring hope where there was once despair. Let us strive to make ourselves available—to God, to one another, and to the countless opportunities that await us each day. For in doing so, we unlock the fullness of life and discover the true meaning of purpose and joy.

Being available makes you a "First Responder," not a "Last Resort." You are there in the good, bad, and the ugly. You are not afraid of the challenges in life, but you show-up every time to face them, and when you do that, you find opportunity to bring resolve.

This will become clearer in the next chapter.

CHAPTER 4

THE ENCOUNTER

"Willingness to adjust our own schedule, agenda, and plans to fit the right desires of God and others. Making personal priorities secondary to the need at hand currently. Reflecting God's priorities so we are always available to Him, and others, when we are serving."
(Dr. Richard Krejoir)

Here we will find examples of people who made themselves available. In *1 Samuel 2-10 (NIV)*, it is recounted that at a certain time, while Eli was lying down in his place, his eyes had begun to grow so dim that he could not see. Take a look into the occasion, *2 One night Eli, whose eyes were becoming so weak that he could barely see, was lying down in his usual place. 3 The lamp of God had not yet gone out, and Samuel was lying down in the house of the Lord, where the ark of God was. 4 Then the Lord called Samuel. Samuel answered, "Here I am." 5 And he ran to Eli and said, "Here I am; you called me." But Eli said, "I did not call; go back and lie down." So he went and lay down.*

6 Again the Lord called, "Samuel!" And Samuel got up and went to Eli and said, "Here I am; you called me." "My son," Eli said, "I did not call; go back and lie down."

7 Now Samuel did not yet know the Lord: The word of the Lord had not yet been revealed to him. 8 A third time the Lord called, "Samuel!" And Samuel got up and went to Eli and said, "Here I am; you called me." Then Eli realized that the Lord was calling the boy. 9 So Eli told Samuel, "Go and lie down, and if he calls you, say, 'Speak, Lord, for your servant is listening.'" So Samuel went and lay down in his place. 10 The Lord came and stood there, calling as at the other times, "Samuel! Samuel!" Then Samuel said, "Speak, for your servant is listening."

This occurred before the lamp of God went out in the Tabernacle of the Lord where the Ark of God was kept. While Samuel was lying down, the Lord called to him. Samuel answered, **"Here I am."** This is akin to saying, **"I'm available."**

So, Samuel ran to Eli and said, "Here I am, for you called me. "Eli responded, "I did not call; go lie down again. "Samuel returned and lay down. The Lord called Samuel again, and Samuel once more went to Eli, saying, "Here I am, for you called me." Eli realized that it was the Lord calling Samuel.

Eli then instructed Samuel, *"Go lie down, and if you are called again, say, "Speak, Lord, for your servant is listening."* (v. 9) Samuel obeyed. When the Lord called again, Samuel responded, *"Speak, for your servant is listening."* (v. 10) Then the Lord revealed a significant message to Samuel concerning events in Israel.

Samuel heard the call, and at least three times he went to Eli, saying, *"Here I am, I'm available."* Being available means saying, "Here I am," indicating readiness and willingness to serve. However, Eli instructed Samuel to direct his availability towards the Lord by saying, "Speak, Lord, for your servant hears." Available people must be skilled, proficient, and accustomed to hearing and conversing with God.

Isaiah 6:8 (NIV), "Then I heard the voice of the Lord saying, "Whom shall I send? And who will go for us?" And I said, "Here am I. Send me!" Isaiah said, *"Here am I. Send me, (in essence) I'm available."*

God seeks individuals who are willing to respond. What would your response be if called upon? Being available sometimes involves mundane tasks, but it's important to respond courageously, just as Isaiah did.

In *Matthew 4:18-20 (NIV)* Jesus called Simon Peter, and Andrew.

18 As Jesus was walking beside the Sea of Galilee, he saw two brothers, Simon called Peter and his brother Andrew. They were casting a net into the lake, for they were fishermen. 19 "Come, follow me," Jesus said, "and I will send you out to fish for people." 20 At once they left their nets and followed him. They immediately made themselves available by following him. They didn't hesitate; they simply responded to the call. This contrasts with the mindset of needing to think about it, which often leads to hesitation and missed opportunities.

In Acts 9:17-19 (NIV) 17 "Then Ananias went to the house and entered it. Placing his hands on Saul, he said, "Brother Saul, the Lord—Jesus, who appeared to you on the road as you were coming here—has sent me so that you may see again and be filled with the Holy Spirit." 18 Immediately, something like scales fell from Saul's eyes, and he could see again. He got up and was baptized, 19 and after taking some food, he regained his strength." We can see here that Ananias made himself available to minister to Saul, who had previously persecuted Christians. Ananias was willing to set aside his doubts and fears to obey God's call. This demonstrates that our gifts and abilities are not just for ourselves but for others, even those we may consider unlikely candidates. Even as you and I anticipate the next move in our business, available people are the first to come into consideration. Available in good times and bad, peak seasons and slow, when praised for what you have done, and when you feel under-valued. Will you still be available?

SELAH *{PAUSE THINK ABOUT IT}*

1. Are you fully present and available to the people and opportunities in your life? If not, what holds you back?

2. How can you make more room for being available to what God or your purpose is calling you to?

3. Reflect on a time when being available changed the course of your day, week, or life. How did it impact you?

CHAPTER 5

TEACHABILITY

Mark 4:25 (AMP)

25 For whoever has [a teachable heart], to him more [understanding] will be given; and whoever does not have [a yearning for truth], even what he has will be taken away from him."

Everybody needs F.A.T. people. But I am not sure if people recognize when they're unteachable. Because everybody believes that they're smart, and intelligent. And kudos because you are that way because God made you that way. The issue is when we attempt to over-think God, and even second guess God. When we start to know better than God. *Proverbs 14:12 (NIV) 12 There is a way that appears to be right, but in the end it leads to death.* The issue? We become God to ourselves. And the Bible's very clear, it says that His mind is so far beyond ours. *Isaiah 55:8-9 (NIV) says, 8 "For my thoughts are not your thoughts, neither are your ways my ways," declares the Lord. 9 "As the heavens are higher than the earth, so are my ways higher than your ways and my thoughts than your thoughts."* His thoughts are so far above ours that we can't even comprehend what He's thinking. How is he going to do it? If we understand that premise, and then hold fast to that premise, then I believe it's important for us to humble ourselves to always be teachable.

When you know it all, nobody can help you. But when you have room to be taught, and a willingness to be taught, then you have positioned yourself to grow. *Hosea 4:6 (NIV) says, my people are destroyed from lack of knowledge. "Because you have rejected knowledge, I also reject you as my priests; because you have ignored the law of your God, I also will ignore your children."* I use this verse to help people understand why I do what I do. The way I do what I do. I don't try to excite people, in the sense of pleasure, because people get a lot of excitement in other places. I believe that we shouldn't have to come to church for excitement. Not that church should be boring, but our "reason" for coming to church should be different. Not because a particular choir is singing; not because a particular speaker is speaking. But when we come to church, we come to church because we want to find out what "Thus says the Lord." What did God say? How does God's word speak to my current situation or prepare me for my future situation? We must be teachable.

Hosea 4:6 says my people are destroyed for lack of knowledge. It says, and it talks about knowledge of the law (the Word of God). God reveals his will in his law, in his Word. If you want to know what the will of God is, you most definitely must get into the Word of God. Look at what he says... *because you, the priestly nation, have rejected knowledge.* Rejection of knowledge is a sign of being unteachable. If I use today's vernacular, it would equate to saying, *"you can't tell me anything."*

Why are the people of God destroyed? Why are the people of God lacking? Why are the people of God not in the place where God would desire them to be? It is simply because they refuse and reject knowledge! If we see ourselves in light of God's Word, it is utterly impossible to stay the same. You must make adjustments. And so, God says, *they rejected knowledge; I will also reject you from being my priest since you have forgotten the law of your God. I will also forget your children.* Maybe the world is the way it is because parents, and those in authority have rejected knowledge and the children are suffering from it; the world is suffering. God says, *I'll reject your children*, not because He does not love your children, but because your children won't even know how to approach Him, or life as it was ordained to be lived. Can you imagine your children missing out in life because "you" rejected the knowledge they would need to be successful? Some people may hear this prophetically, if our children don't know how to approach God, what is God to do? Just bless anyway, anyhow? No, that's the gravity, the importance, and seriousness of reality. I sense in the spirit that people are saying, *"well, pastor, I am not a priest."* But I want to beg to differ.

1 Peter 2:9 (NKJV) says, But you are a chosen generation, a royal priesthood, a holy nation, His own special people, that you may proclaim the praises of Him who called you out of darkness into His marvelous light". And there it is! A holy nation and royal priesthood. Now, think about this for a second. Rejection of knowledge doesn't only happen in the church. We reject knowledge in our jobs, and knowledge in our families. For example, our parents spend most of our early years expressing what it will take to grow into independence. If we rejected what they were saying to us, we may still be living with our parents. We rejected the knowledge being given. I know there are exceptions, but can you identify? Have you ever thought that your mother or your father just didn't know what they were talking about because **times have changed**, and so, even what they were telling you at the time you rejected? Most young people did or do! It is human nature that we reject knowledge for some reason. Think about this, *Isaiah 30:1 (NKJV) "Woe to the rebellious children," says the Lord, "Who take counsel, but not of Me, And who devise plans, but not of My Spirit..."* Children not wanting anyone to tell them anything is nothing new is it?

Now, we've covered two very important characteristics. The first one was being faithful. And the second, is available. Now, these two characteristics are necessary, but they are nothing if you're not teachable.

You can't be faithful if you're not teachable. You won't be available if you are not teachable. One builds on the other. Teachable means *being capable*; and your capacity is developed by your ability, and receptiveness *of being taught*. "Am I capable of being taught?" is the question you must ask yourself.

Teachable means "willing to learn," and capable of being taught with a willingness to learn. When is it ample time or the right time to stop learning? I'm an advocate for the saying, *you should only stop learning when you die*. If you are alive, you should be learning something. It doesn't matter if you are 150 years old, you still won't know it all.

Someone should be able to teach you new things. How to work on a computer, or a new software program, an iPhone, a smart TV, or something else. I believe that you will agree with me and say *yes, I can learn, and I have the willingness! B*ut the question becomes; when you look at your daily routine, are you developing the capacity, and are you willing? What good is the capacity if you're not willing? A bottle can hold water, but if I don't put water in it, what good is it? What do you do with an empty bottle? How useful are you when you are constantly present and available, yet your capacity cannot fulfill its potential for use? To be teachable is more than gathering information. It is exercising humility, willingness, and the ability to become pliable in situations, even if there is a lack of interest or excitement. I must equip myself enough and be willing to "receive" this information. After I have humbled myself to receive this information, there's another step that exemplifies being pliable; being moldable.

Now, your critics are going to tell you, when you are being molded, you are being brainwashed. I would say, when you become, or are pliable in situations, you are being conformed. We as Christians, as believers, ought to be conformed to the image of Christ. The Bible says, *in Philippians 2:5 (NKJV) "Let this mind be in you which was also in Christ Jesus".* Be teachable - conformity won't come if you don't receive the information. Being pliable won't happen if you don't receive the knowledge. Begin to say, "I have this humility because I understand, and I am willing to learn." Sometimes, even if we can't see the end from the beginning, if we take the knowledge that we have at the moment, it'll get us closer to the end.

Being teachable is important. It's important in life because it allows you to learn new things, engage in new conversations, and solve problems that you would've never been able to solve, or engage in otherwise. In other words, if you can't learn certain things, you can't solve certain problems. If I can't learn how electricity works, you may not be able to get the light back on. That's why the Bible says, *Wisdom is the principle thing; Therefore get wisdom. And in all your getting, get understanding. Proverbs 4:7 (NKJV)* Only people who are teachable gain understanding. Are you teachable?

If you are a teachable person, you make every effort to grow, and you ask for feedback. These are some of the things teachable people do.

One of the most intimidating times in my family is when we sit around a table, and I ask people what they think about a matter. Boy, oh boy, you don't know!

Even around the table, folks think differently. In other words, once I ask for this feedback, I've got to absorb it like a sponge. I must receive it and adjust accordingly. It's all a part of being teachable.

Someone who's teachable looks at the other person's opinions as valuable learning tools, not as negative criticism. Just because people have a different opinion doesn't mean they're criticizing you negatively. Here's something John Maxwell said, *"Teachability is not so much about competence and mental capacity as it is about attitude. It is the desire to listen, learn, and apply. It is the hunger to discover and grow teachability. It is the willingness to learn, unlearn and relearn."* Because some of the lessons you have learned, if it is not applicable in a certain situation, you would do yourself good to unlearn it. But be open enough or willing enough to relearn, so you can be effective in the current situation.

Have you ever wondered why people in the kingdom of God suffer the way they do? It is simply because they don't pursue knowledge. For example, it's an indictment on the church when you have 30,000 members and you can't get 200 for Bible Study. 200 sounds like a large number, but it only sounds like a large number to a small church. But if you take 30,000 members and you can only get 200, that's telling you that there's another 29,800 that don't want to be in a teaching environment (exceptions noted). It didn't just start. People say, *"well, I'm working, I can't do it Wednesday and Sunday. I'm here on Sunday."* Okay, well, why is it that Sunday School Class only has a few members, or no longer exists, but at the 10 o'clock Worship Service, you can't find a place to park?

Allow me to submit that most Believers would rather "catch the spirit" as opposed to *"walk in the spirit," Gal. 5:16 (NKJV)* It didn't just start. Being teachable is a soft skill. It is a unique trait that often makes or breaks an effective person. It is recognizing that even though you may have a particular skill, you are capable of receiving more information, which will allow you to become more effective and efficient in what you do.

We must grow to be in a place where we always have this mindset. So, reposition yourself to where you are willing to listen, to learn, to grow, and to hear so that you can be more efficient and effective. The moment we can accept the fact that we are not perfect, we can open ourselves up to learning more. Can you admit; I'm not perfect, my kids are not perfect, my job is not perfect, the people I work with are not perfect, nobody is perfect. So, if I can accept my imperfections, then I can accept other people's imperfections too. If you find that there always seems to be something wrong with everyone else, and there's rarely anything wrong with you, you may not be teachable.

It's always somebody else's fault. A person who thinks they're perfect just the way they are feels there is no reason to be taught. That's the truth. Especially by somebody who's imperfect. They feel, "what are you going to tell me if you aren't perfect? If you aren't put together?" If nothing else, you should learn from their imperfections.

Being ignorant about a thing is not bad, it is only when you are ignorant, and nobody can teach you anything that ignorance becomes bad.

Do you realize how many times in the New Testament, Paul came to the people of God and said, ***"Brethren, I would not have you ignorant concerning these things." 1 Thessalonians 4:13; Romans. 11:25;***

1 Corinthians 12:1 (NKJV) Now, if the ignorant person told Paul, "how can you tell me that whereas you persecuted us before you got here? I was here before you." Then, they would not have learned anything from Paul. And I know that it's hard to believe, but there are some people that you just can't tell anything to anymore. That's the urgency, or the seriousness of the accusation, but it's so true.

Can you understand how this mindset plays into where we are in life? If your teachers didn't teach you, you would have dropped out, and if you quit, you still must survive. Living life from a position of ignorance about how things should be developing makes life difficult. Now, you must figure out how you are going to survive. So you seek some "street knowledge," because deep down you realize that you "know" what to do, so the street becomes your teacher. What the street teaches you carries heavier consequences than what the school of wise instructors would teach you. You can talk about street knowledge all you want, but it is real, and the consequences are heavy - it's heavy on both sides. The consequences are heavy in the street and while you are in the street. But the consequences are also heavy if you get caught "dirty" in the street, and with your street knowledge the consequences are still the same.

The street will be hard on you and the system too. To have a teachable spirit about yourself, not just in church, but wherever you find yourself is paramount.

Don't even go to the movies if the usher can't tell you where to sit, it's just a mindset. If I have this mind that nobody can tell me anything, then it follows me wherever I go. And it expresses itself, even unconsciously. Be Teachable in all that you do, please!

When we are unwilling to learn, it is at that point in life that we are no longer teachable. As a result, the ability to grow, expand, and receive promotion ends. *Mark 4:25 (AMP) 25 For whoever has [a teachable heart], to him more [understanding] will be given; and whoever does not have [a yearning for truth], even what he has will be taken away from him."*

CHAPTER 6

MAXIMIZING OPPORTUNITIES

"Embrace the unknown, for in it lies the greatest opportunities for growth."
(Author Unknown)

Opportunities are like sunrises, a gift from above that illuminates the path to growth and progress. In the Word of God, we see numerous examples of individuals who seized opportunities presented to them, often amidst adversity and uncertainty.

Consider the story of Joseph in the Old Testament. Despite being sold into slavery by his brothers and facing numerous trials and tribulations, Joseph remained faithful to God and maintained a teachable spirit. When presented with the opportunity to interpret Pharaoh's dreams, Joseph didn't hesitate to use his God-given wisdom and insight. By interpreting the dreams accurately, Joseph not only saved Egypt from famine but also positioned himself for a remarkable rise to power and influence.

Another biblical example is the story of Esther. As an orphaned Jewish girl raised by her cousin Mordecai, Esther found herself thrust into a position of influence when she became queen of Persia.

Esther 4:12-14(NIV) 12 When Esther's words were reported to Mordecai, 13 he sent back this answer: "Do not think that because you are in the king's house you alone of all the Jews will escape. 14 For if you remain silent at this time, relief and deliverance for the Jews will arise from another place, but you and your father's family will perish. And who knows but that you have come to your royal position for such a time as this?"

When Mordecai uncovered a plot to annihilate the Jewish people, he urged Esther to use her position to intercede on behalf of her people. Despite the risks involved, Esther seized the opportunity and approached the king, risking her own life to plead for the salvation of her people.

Through her bravery and courage, Esther not only saved her people but also secured their safety for generations to come.

Furthermore, the parable of the talents in Matthew 25 (previously referenced) illustrates the importance of seizing opportunities and using our God-given gifts wisely. In this parable, a master entrusts his servants with varying amounts of talent before going on a journey. Upon his return, he evaluates their stewardship of the talents. The servants who invested their talents wisely and seized growth opportunities were rewarded, while the one who buried his talent out of fear was rebuked. This parable illustrates the importance of seizing opportunities for growth and maximizing our potential for the glory of God.

In life, opportunities will always come to every man, but they come in seasons. King Solomon said in *Ecclesiastes 9:11b (NKJV) that one thing is common to all men is "time and chance."* Time here represents opportunities, while chance represents seasons. You will always get opportunities; however, you can only maximize the opportunities when you are prepared for them beforehand. When you are F.A.T., maximizing each opportunity will be a possibility and proven evident.

Consider David. He was F.A.T. while in the wilderness taking care of his father's sheep, he was faithful, he never allowed even one sheep kept under his care to be devoured by wild animals.

He was teachable, he kept learning about God, loving God, and learning to play stringed instruments excellently and spiritually.

When King Saul needed someone to play music for him, David was recommended and he was ready and made himself available to the opportunity. Being F.A.T brought him to the palace.

Again, when Goliath was ranting and cursing the God of Israel, David knew that what God was seeking at that point was a man who would make himself available to be used by God. From what he had "learned" and experienced about God; he seized that opportunity. David knew how to bring God into a battle, he knew that when he put God in front, and channels the glory to Him, He will arise and take over the battle. It was teachability that afforded him that knowledge.

The story ends with God empowering David with wisdom to fight the battle with a slingshot and stones, killing Goliath. David said to Goliath in *1 Samuel 17:45 (NKJV) "You come to me with a sword, with a spare and with a javelin. But I come to you in the name of the Lord of hosts, the God of the armies of Israel, whom you have defied"* David was only an available instrument in God's hands. How can a stone sink into a skull as big as that of Goliath as though it was a bullet? How come Goliath fell face down instead of backwards? He bowed to the God who killed him, whom he insulted and challenged to a fight.

In our own lives, opportunities may come disguised as challenges, setbacks, or even failures. It is our faithfulness, availability, and teachability that enable us to recognize and seize these opportunities when they arise.

As we remain faithful to God, make ourselves available for His purposes, and maintain a teachable spirit, we position ourselves to embrace opportunities for growth, success, and fulfillment.

Selah

{Pause think about it}

1. Are you open to receiving correction or guidance from others? Why or why not?

2. What's the most recent lesson life has taught you, and how have you applied it?

3. How can you cultivate a more teachable spirit in areas where you tend to resist change or new ideas?

CHAPTER 7

THE NEED FOR WISDOM

James 1:5 (NIV)

5 If any of you lacks wisdom, you should ask God, who gives generously to all without finding fault, and it will be given to you.

Wisdom, often portrayed as a precious jewel in the Word of God, is the cornerstone of a fulfilling and purposeful life. Throughout the pages of Scripture, we encounter individuals who exemplify the pursuit and application of wisdom in their lives.

Such as Solomon, renowned for his wisdom and discernment. Solomon humbly approached God and asked for wisdom to govern His people with justice and righteousness.

2 Chronicles 1:7-12 (NIV)

7 That night God appeared to Solomon and said to him, "Ask for whatever you want me to give you."

8 Solomon answered God, "You have shown great kindness to David my father and have made me king in his place. 9 Now, Lord God, let your promise to my father David be confirmed, for you have made me king over a people who are as numerous as the dust of the earth. 10 Give me wisdom and knowledge, that I may lead this people, for who is able to govern this great people of yours?"

11 God said to Solomon, "Since this is your heart's desire and you have not asked for wealth, possessions or honor, nor for the death of your enemies, and since you have not asked for a long life but for wisdom and knowledge to govern my people over whom I have made you king, 12 therefore wisdom and knowledge will be given you. And I will also give you wealth, possessions and honor, such as no king who was before you ever had and none after you will have."

Impressed by Solomon's request, God granted him not only wisdom but also wealth and honor beyond measure. Solomon's reign was characterized by unparalleled wisdom and prosperity, attracting visitors from far and wide to seek his counsel and marvel at his accomplishments.

The book of Proverbs, attributed to Solomon is a treasure trove of timeless wisdom and practical insights. *Proverbs 1:7 (NIV) declares, The fear of the Lord is the beginning of knowledge, but fools despise wisdom and instruction.* Throughout Proverbs, Solomon imparts wisdom on topics ranging from diligence and integrity to humility and discernment. He emphasizes the importance of seeking wisdom above all else and applying it diligently in every aspect of life.

In the New Testament, Jesus Himself is hailed as the embodiment of wisdom. In *Luke 2:52 (NIV)*, we are told that Jesus *"grew in wisdom and stature, and in favor with God and man."* Throughout His earthly ministry, Jesus demonstrated unparalleled wisdom in His teachings, parables, and interactions with others. He challenged conventional wisdom, exposed hypocrisy, and revealed the true essence of God's kingdom.

Moreover, the apostle James exhorts believers, *If any of you lacks wisdom, you should ask God, who gives generously to all without finding fault, and it will be given to you. James 1:5 (NIV).* He contrasts earthly wisdom, characterized by selfish ambition and jealousy, with heavenly wisdom, marked by purity, peace, and humility.

In our own lives, the pursuit of wisdom requires humility, diligence, and a willingness to learn from both successes and failures by instruction. As we meditate on God's Word, seek His guidance in prayer, and surround ourselves with wise counsel, we grow in wisdom and discernment. May we heed the timeless wisdom found in Scripture and apply it faithfully in our daily lives, glorifying God and blessing those around us.

CONCLUSION

"Are You F.A.T.?" offers a transformative journey toward personal growth, spiritual maturity, and fulfillment. Through exploring the principles of faithfulness, availability, and teachability, my prayer is, readers are challenged to reassess their priorities, attitudes, and actions considering timeless biblical truths. "Are You F.A.T." emphasizes the importance of remaining faithful to God's call, making ourselves available for His purposes and maintaining a teachable spirit that is open to learning and growth.

As we reflect on the stories of biblical figures and their encounters with faith, opportunity, and wisdom, we are inspired to emulate their examples and apply their lessons to our lives. Whether it's Joseph's resilience in the face of adversity, Esther's courage amid danger, or Solomon's pursuit of wisdom above all else, each narrative serves as a poignant reminder of the transformative power of faith and obedience.

Furthermore, "Are You F.A.T.?" challenges you to seize the opportunities that come your way, recognizing them as divine appointments orchestrated by a loving and sovereign God. By embracing opportunities for growth, service, and impact, you are empowered to fulfill your God-given potential and make a meaningful difference in the world around you.

Ultimately, "Are You F.A.T." underscores the timeless truth that true fulfillment and success are found in aligning our lives with God's purposes and principles.

As you cultivate a lifestyle of faithfulness, availability, and teachability, you position yourself to experience the abundant life that God promises to those who follow Him wholeheartedly. May "Are You F.A.T.?" catalyze spiritual growth, personal development, and a deeper walk with God for all who embark on this transformative journey wherever you find yourself.

ABOUT THE AUTHOR

Pastor R. Dave Jones is a native of New Orleans, LA. He now resides in Lithonia, Georgia. He is a graduate of the Beulah Heights Bible College, in Atlanta, GA where he received a Bachelor of Arts degree in Biblical Education.

Pastor Jones began his service to the Lord through the gift of singing, which he did for many years throughout the country. In 1982, he began to study God's Word and started teaching Sunday School which he continued to do until 1986, when God called him into the five- fold ministry; after which he began to "proclaim and teach" God's Word. Unsure of all that God had in store for him, he faithfully assisted other Pastors with Evangelism, Outreach Ministries, New Members' Classes, Bible Studies, Seminars and Conferences.

He is the Pastor of Beacon Light Christian Center. His teaching gift comes as a result of what God spoke into his spirit from Hosea 4:6a, "My people are destroyed for the lack of knowledge".

His joy and delight is to see people become born-again believers and mature by the Word of God. As he continues to minister to the Body of

Christ, his desire is for believers, leaders, and laymen to mature in their lifestyle, conversation, and demonstration in the Holy Spirit. This includes their responsibility, accountability and service to the Lord and men.

Pastor Jones could not do all he does without the help of his family, Beatrice F. Jones, wife and partner in ministry, Serena J. Dorsey, favorite oldest daughter, Sonya Jones, favorite youngest daughter, grandchildren Nia Shantrell, Danielle Nicole, and Dorian Dave, Loretta A. Richardson, his sister, and the faithful members of Beacon Light Christian Center. Even though, he is indebted to all these people, **all the Glory goes to God!**

Made in the USA
Columbia, SC
24 October 2024

44570669R00035